DIG DEEP!
Bugs That Live
Underground

Termites

Liz Chung

PowerKiDS
press

New York

Published in 2017 by The Rosen Publishing Group, Inc.
29 East 21st Street, New York, NY 10010

First Edition

Editor: Sarah Machajewski
Book Design: Mickey Harmon

Photo Credits: Cover (sky) Severe/Shutterstock.com; cover (background) ifong/Shutterstock.com; cover (termites) sydeen/Shutterstock.com; pp. 3–4, 6, 8, 10, 12, 14, 16, 18, 20, 22–24 (background) isaravut/Shutterstock.com; p. 5 Dr. Morley Read/Shutterstock.com; p. 7 Cheng Wei/Shutterstock.com; p. 8 NaibankFotos/Shutterstock.com; p. 9 Igor Kolos/Shutterstock.com; p. 11 Byelikova Oksana/Shutterstock.com; p. 13 (cross-section) Dorling Kindersley/Getty Images; p. 13 (background) Raduga11/Shutterstock.com; p. 15 Gregory MD./Science Source/Getty Images; p. 17 wonderisland/Shutterstock.com; p. 19 Decha Thapanya/Shutterstock.com; p. 21 InsectWorld/Shutterstock.com; p. 22 khazari/Shutterstock.com.

Cataloging-in-Publication Data

Names: Chung, Liz.
Title: Termites / Liz Chung.
Description: New York : PowerKids Press, 2017. | Series: Dig deep! bugs that live underground | Includes index.
Identifiers: ISBN 9781499420623 (pbk.) | ISBN 9781499420647 (library bound) | ISBN 9781499420630 (6 pack)
Subjects: LCSH: Termites–Juvenile literature.
Classification: LCC QL529.C58 2017| DDC 595.7'36–dc23

Manufactured in the United States of America

CPSIA Compliance Information: Batch #BS16PK: For Further Information contact Rosen Publishing, New York, New York at 1-800-237-9932

Contents

The Terrible Termite

Most people don't like termites. These **insects** are known to cause major damage, or harm, to homes, other buildings, and pretty much anything else made of wood. Unfortunately, termites can be tough to get rid of once they make it into a building's walls. Termites live in huge groups that can have millions of members, and they make new termites all the time.

Surprisingly, termites aren't all bad. Many species, or kinds, live underground instead of inside wood. These termites keep the soil in their **ecosystems** healthy. Let's dig into the world of termites—they're actually pretty cool!

Some termites spend most of their lives underground. Some live inside rotting wood and walls.

Around the World

Scientists know of about 2,750 termite species. Termites are common bugs, and they live in many parts of the world. They're found in Europe, Asia, Africa, Australia, South America, and North America. Generally, termites don't live where it's really cold.

Some termite species have made their way around the world because of people. People have accidentally carried termites to new places in furniture, boats, lumber, and wooden crates. They survive the journey because they can go for long periods without any water. Termites that live underground can survive outside soil as long as there's water available.

Dig Deeper!

A North American termite species may have been accidentally carried into the Royal Palace in Vienna in crates that held potted plants.

Once termites arrive in a place, they're often there to stay. They set up their nests and multiply quickly.

Three Types of Termites

There are three general types of termites—subterranean, dry-wood, and **damp**-wood. "Subterranean" means "under the surface of the earth." This type of termite needs to be in contact with the soil to survive. Subterranean termites can live in fallen trees, tree stumps, dead wood, or any wood that's touching soil. This can include homes and buildings.

Damp-wood termites live in **decaying** wood that's wet from water leaks or soil. Dry-wood termites live in dry wood, such as fences, stairs, furniture, decks, and walls. Their nests are above ground and never touch the soil.

Dig Deeper!

Dry-wood termites are the most destructive, or harmful, kind of termite.

The holes in this wood are a sure sign termites were there.

Nests from the Outside

Termites live in nests, which they build either in the soil or above the ground in wood. Nests are built from dirt, tiny pieces of clay, and tiny pieces of wood. As termites build, they use their own waste and spit to glue the pieces of the nest in place.

Termite nests are closed off from the outside world except for openings the termites use to enter and exit their home. Termite nests are often hidden, which keeps the termites safe from predators and people who may want to get rid of them. However, some kinds of termites build huge nests above ground.

Dig Deeper!

Termite nests look solid, but their walls are covered with tiny holes, called pores, that allow air to get in.

Termites in Africa and Australia build aboveground nests that can be between 10 and 30 feet (3 and 9.1 m) tall! These nests have hard walls, chimneys, and many rooms and tunnels inside.

Inside the Nest

A termite nest can be very **complex**. Inside, there is an organized network of tunnels and galleries, or rooms. The galleries are used to store food, keep eggs safe, and house the queen termite. Worker termites are always building and repairing the tunnels and galleries.

The inside of a termite nest is warm, damp, and dark. The **temperature** inside is usually higher than the temperature outside. Termites build covered runways called mud tubes to and from the nest. Mud tubes help maintain the warm and damp conditions termites need to survive. They are a sign that a termite nest is nearby.

Dig Deeper!

Some termites grow a kind of **fungus** inside their nest. Termites eat the fungus, which helps their body **digest** wood.

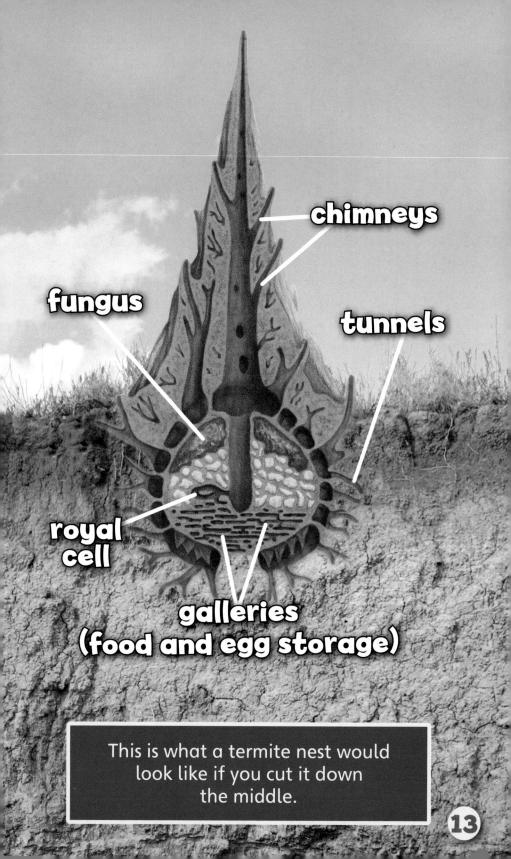

chimneys

fungus

tunnels

royal cell

galleries
(food and egg storage)

This is what a termite nest would look like if you cut it down the middle.

Building a Colony

Termites are very social bugs. They live in groups called colonies. Some termite colonies have millions of members, but a colony starts with just two termites. A male and a female termite find a nesting site in soil or wood. The female lays a small number of eggs at first. The colony matures in two to five years.

Colonies have a caste, or class, system. The major castes are reproductive termites, soldier termites, and worker termites. Each has a special job to do. A termite's caste is determined as it grows from a **larva** into an adult. Let's explore a termite's life cycle.

Every termite has a job that helps the colony survive.

Life Begins

The termites that start a colony are the king and queen. They alone produce all the termites living in a colony, and they can live to be 60 to 70 years old! Queen termites are huge, with a very large **abdomen** that's designed for egg laying.

Mature queens can lay up to 36,000 eggs a day. The eggs hatch into pale larvae called nymphs. Termites molt, or shed their skin, as they grow into adults. The king and queen take care of the first nymphs by feeding them and caring for the nest. However, the nymphs or workers take over these jobs as the colony grows.

Dig Deeper!

Winged termites fly to a nesting site where they mate and lay eggs. They shed their wings after they land.

queen termite

Queens can be so big that they can't move. Sometimes they can grow up to 4.3 inches (11 cm) long!

Workers and Soldiers

The first nymphs in a colony develop into soldiers and workers. They don't have wings and they usually don't have eyes. The biggest group in a termite colony is usually the worker class. They're pale and their body is soft. They have mouthparts designed for chewing. It's the workers' job to build the nest, find food, feed the other termites, and care for the eggs.

Soldier termites **protect** the colony. They have a big, dark head and powerful jaws that can have teeth. Soldier termites can leap toward a predator (such as an ant) and open and close their jaws around it. Since they're blind, soldier termites find their enemies by touch and smell.

Dig Deeper!

One kind of soldier termite has a long **snout** that can shoot a clear, sticky liquid at predators.

A termite's caste is based on what the colony needs. If it's short on workers, termite nymphs will develop into workers.

soldier termite

worker termites

Taking Flight

Winged reproductive termites are called alates. They have hard, dark bodies, eyes, and a pair of wings, which they lose after they land. Alates are the termites that leave the nest, mate, and start a new colony.

Reproductive termites leave the nest in swarms, or large numbers. Swarming time depends on the species. Some termites swarm after it's rained a lot, while others swarm in the late summer. Most alates are eaten by predators when they leave the nest. Birds, lizards, ants, and other bugs are common termite predators.

Dig Deeper!

If a king or queen is sick or dies, the termite colony makes a new reproductive to replace it. This new king or queen is called a secondary reproductive.

Reproductive termites are often mistaken for winged ants. Can you see why?

Looking for Clues

    Termite colonies can survive for many years. Most termites never come above ground—they stay safe underground or inside wooden structures. If they find their way inside our homes, it's not usually something we can see. They use their expertly made tunnels to pass in and out without being seen.

    Even though we don't usually see termites, they leave clues about their presence. Piles of sawdust or mud tubes are signs termites are close by. Holes in wood are a sign, too. Sometimes we see winged adults when they swarm. If you do see termites, let someone know. It's important they don't get inside!

Glossary

abdomen: The part of the body that contains the stomach.

complex: Made of many parts.

damp: Slightly wet.

decay: To rot.

digest: To break down food inside the body so that the body can use it.

ecosystem: A community of living creatures.

fungus: A living thing that is somewhat like a plant but doesn't make its own food or have leaves or a green color. Fungi include molds and mushrooms.

insect: A small animal that has six legs and one or two pairs of wings.

larva: A stage in an insect's life between the egg and the adult stage. The plural form is "larvae."

protect: To keep safe.

snout: In termites, a part of the head that sticks out, much like a nose.

temperature: How hot or cold something is

Index

A
alates, 20

C
caste, 14, 19
colonies, 14, 16, 18, 19, 20, 22

D
damp-wood termites, 8
dry-wood termites, 8

E
eggs, 12, 13, 14, 16, 18

F
fungus, 12, 13

G
galleries, 12, 13

L
larva, 14, 16

M
mud tubes, 12, 22

N
nests, 7, 8, 10, 11, 12, 13, 16, 18, 20
nymphs, 16, 18, 19

P
predators, 10, 18, 20

Q
queen, 12, 16, 17, 20

R
reproductive termites, 14, 20, 21

S
soldier termites, 14, 18, 19
species, 4, 6, 20
subterranean termites, 8
swarms, 20, 22

W
wings, 16, 18, 20, 21, 22
worker termites, 12, 14, 16, 18, 19

Websites

Due to the changing nature of Internet links, PowerKids Press has developed an online list of websites related to the subject of this book. This site is updated regularly. Please use this link to access the list: www.powerkidslinks.com/digd/term